CHRISTMA
SONGS FOR THE RECORDER

PUBLISHED COMPLETE WITH LYRICS AND GUITAR DIAGRAMS
PLUS A TWO PAGE INTRODUCTION TO PLAYING THE RECORDER

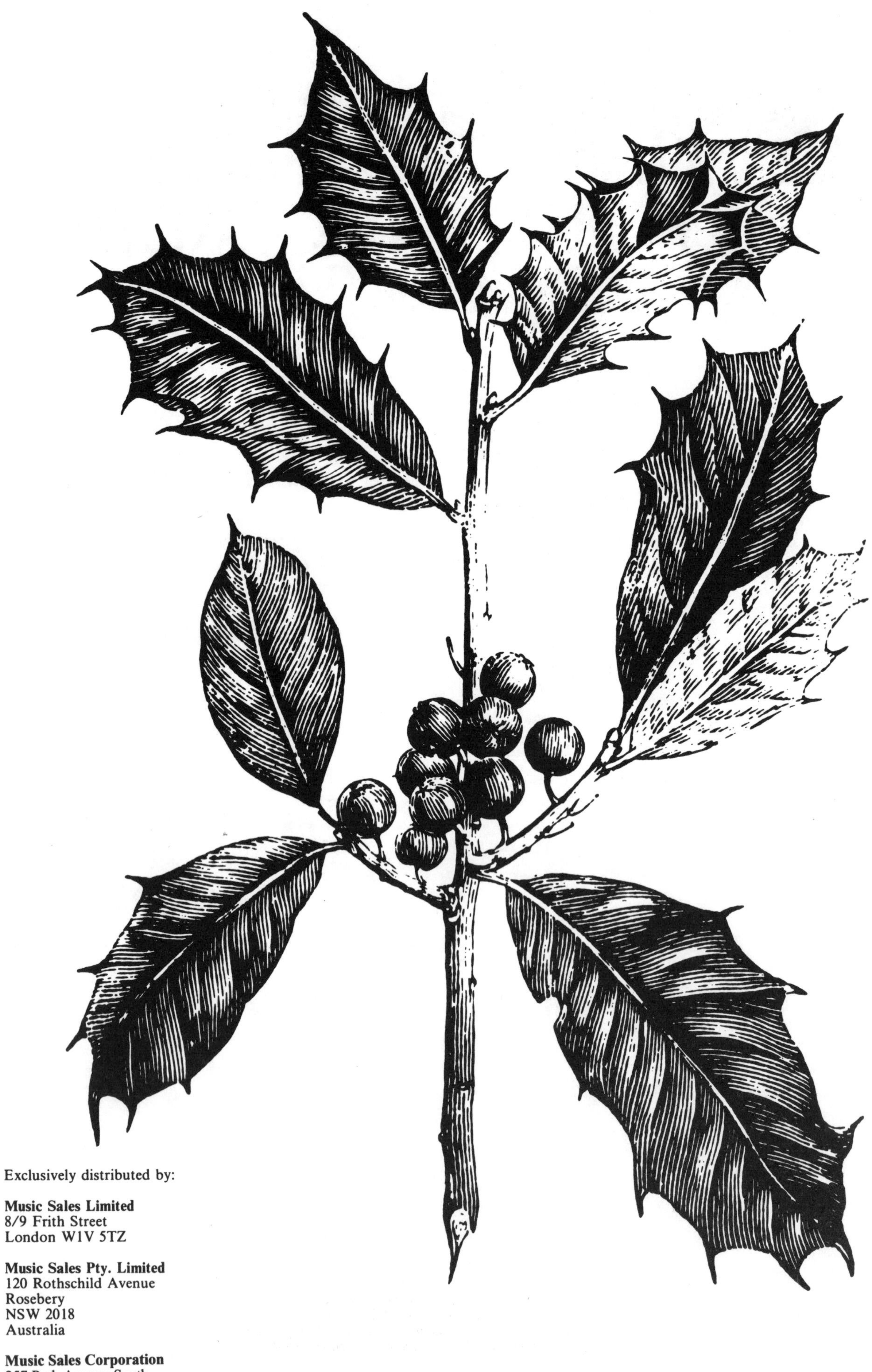

Exclusively distributed by:

Music Sales Limited
8/9 Frith Street
London W1V 5TZ

Music Sales Pty. Limited
120 Rothschild Avenue
Rosebery
NSW 2018
Australia

Music Sales Corporation
257 Park Avenue South,
New York,
NY 10010, U.S.A.

Contents

Playing and Care of the Recorder

HOLDING THE RECORDER

The recorder has eight holes, seven on the front and one in the rear. It is held with the left hand on the top portion and the right hand on the lower. The left thumb covers the rear hole and the other fingers follow as shown in the accompanying diagram.

Each finger covers only the hole assigned to it, and no other. This never varies. The right thumb is used only to support the instrument and the left little finger is not used at all.

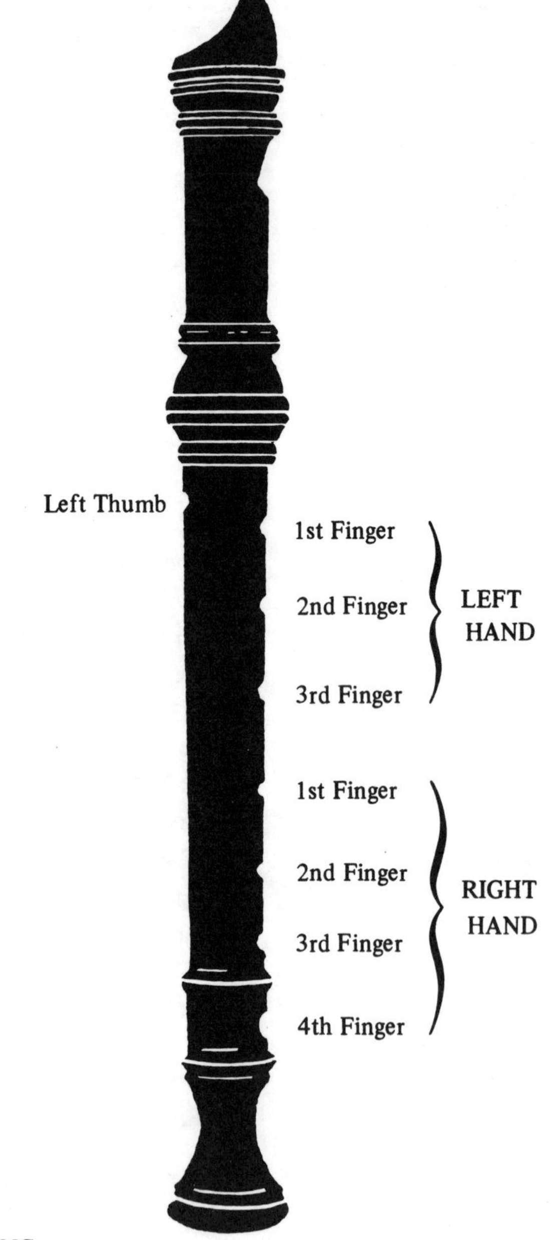

FINGERING DIAGRAM

LEFT HAND

Left thumb hole O   O 1st finger

O 2nd finger

O 3rd finger

RIGHT HAND

O 1st finger

O 2nd finger

O 3rd finger

O 4th finger

When hole is:

○	= do not finger
●	= close completely
◐	= open
◒	= left thumbhole pinched (approximately 7/10 closed)

FINGERING

Fingering the recorder should be done firmly, yet not with heavy pressure. When a hole is to be covered, it must be covered completely. The finger tips are not used, but rather the soft pads of the fingers. Fingers not in use should be kept about one half inch above the holes to which they are assigned, and when called into play should fall like little hammers and with gentle force.

The recorder is supported by the lips and right thumb. The right thumb is positioned approximately behind the first finger of the right hand. The recorder is held to the lips at a 45 degree angle. The elbows are held away from the body, slightly forward and up.

BREATHING

Blowing through the recorder must be done with an even and constant breath pressure. This is so important that you would do well to re-read and commit this to memory.

Should you increase the breath pressure while playing, the tone will become higher (sharp) and if diminished, the tone will become lower (flat). The result will be an out of tune performance.

The proper pressure to produce a good tone will vary. In general, the lower tones require less pressure than the middle range, while the higher tones need a stronger pressure. However, whatever pressure used, it must be kept constant for the duration of the note.

Breathing spots are marked in the music with the symbol:

,

A breath is also taken at a rest, double bar, repeat sign.

TONGUING

Tonguing is a device for starting and stopping a tone and giving the sound definition. It is one of the most important recorder techniques to understand and develop correctly from the start.

The recorder mouthpiece is placed between the lips with a slight grip. The teeth and tongue never touch the instrument. Let your tongue find the ridge in your upper mouth about where the teeth go into the gums. With the recorder between the lips and tongue in position, softly say the syllable "DAH". Do this several times in succession, and the last time say "DAH - d". Do this until it becomes automatic.

What you have done would look like this:

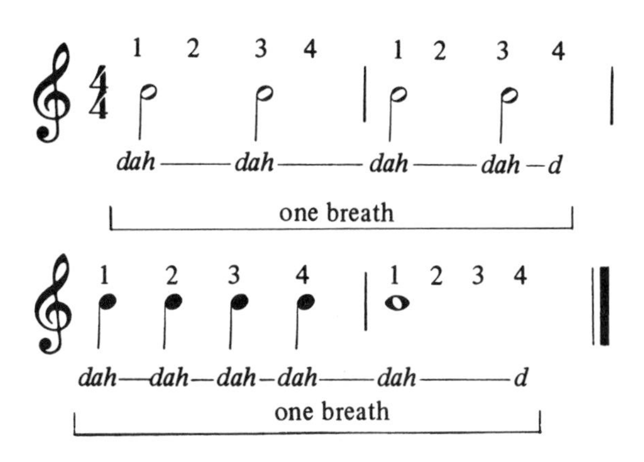

STACCATO has the effect of shortening the duration of a note. The shortness of the note will depend upon the character of the piece.

Staccato notes are indicated by dots over the notes. Tonguing is slightly different for staccato and looks like this:

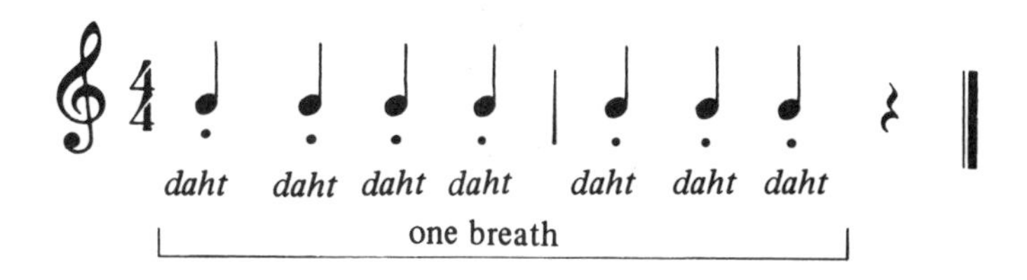

LEGATO is indicated by a curved line connecting two or more different tones. The first note in the slur is tongued with DAH - the AH sound is maintained for the other notes within the slur, and the last note in the slur is ended with the final 'd' sound. It looks like this:

Where there are other notes following and not included in the slur, and no breath marks or rest occur, the final 'd' is omitted from the slur until called for:

CARE OF THE RECORDER

Before playing your recorder, warm the mouthpiece in your hand. This will help hold moisture condensation in the windway to a minimum.

Most recorders are furnished with a swab. If yours is not, use a soft piece of cloth on a stick and wipe out the instrument after each playing. Be careful not to touch the delicate lip in the window. Damage to the lip will alter the tone.

When assembling the parts use a slow twisting motion to avoid forcing and damaging the joints.

If the joints become loose, wrap them with transparent tape. If they become tight, rub them with a light grease.

If moisture collects in the windway while playing, hold your finger over the slot and blow the moisture out.

Wooden recorders should be treated with the care given any delicate piece of wood. They should not be exposed to extremes of heat or cold.

Read and follow the direction sheet enclosed with most recorders.

TUNING THE RECORDER

Instruments may vary slightly in pitch. For group playing, close tuning is desired. Have each person sound B. Listen carefully for the lowest sounding B. Then each recorder may be lowered in pitch by twisting it apart at the top (tuning) joint, thereby lengthening the instrument. Shorten and lengthen each recorder by small adjustments until all are tuned to the lowest B.

B

Recorder Fingering Chart

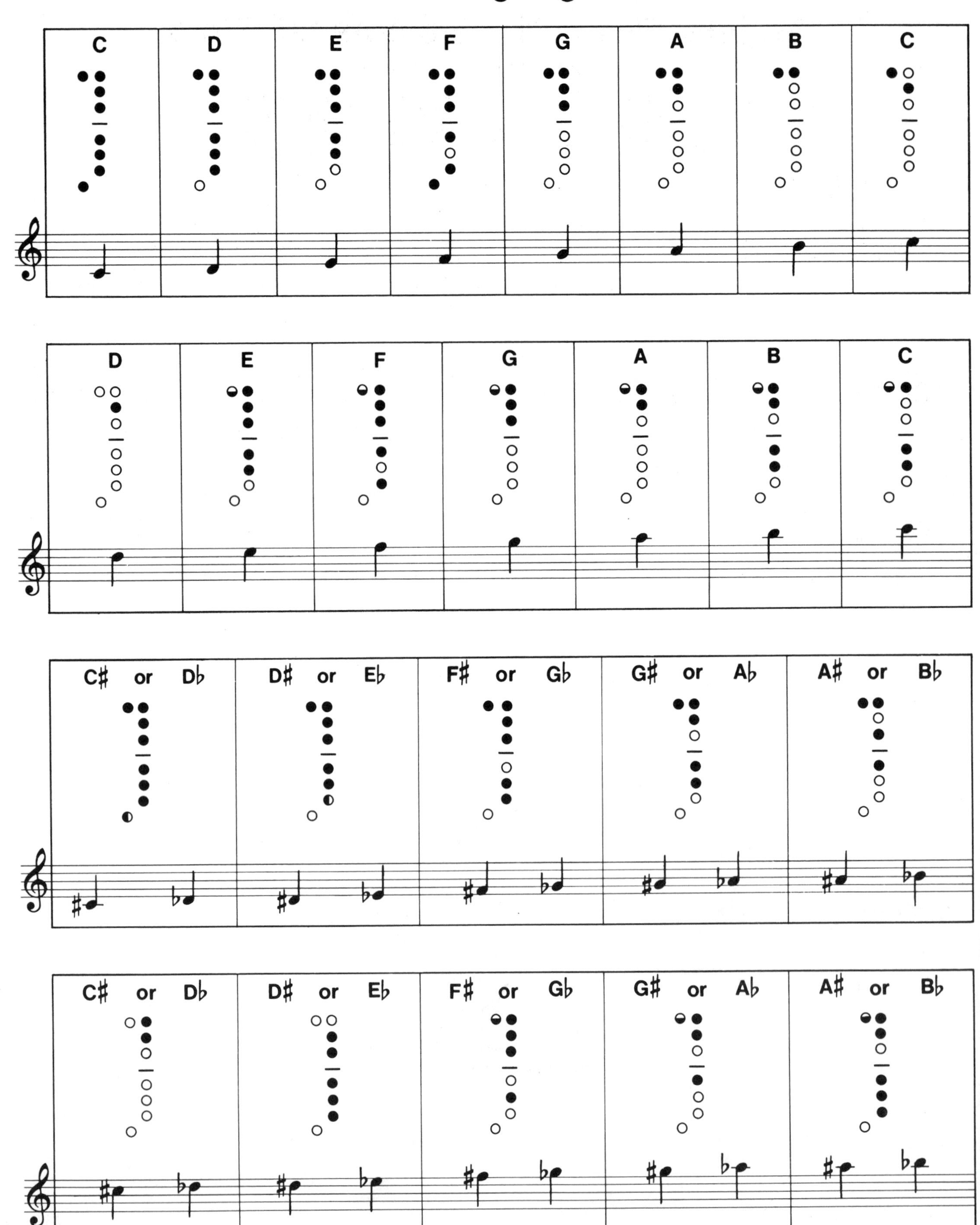

Angels, From The Realms Of Glory

CHORDS USED IN THIS CAROL:

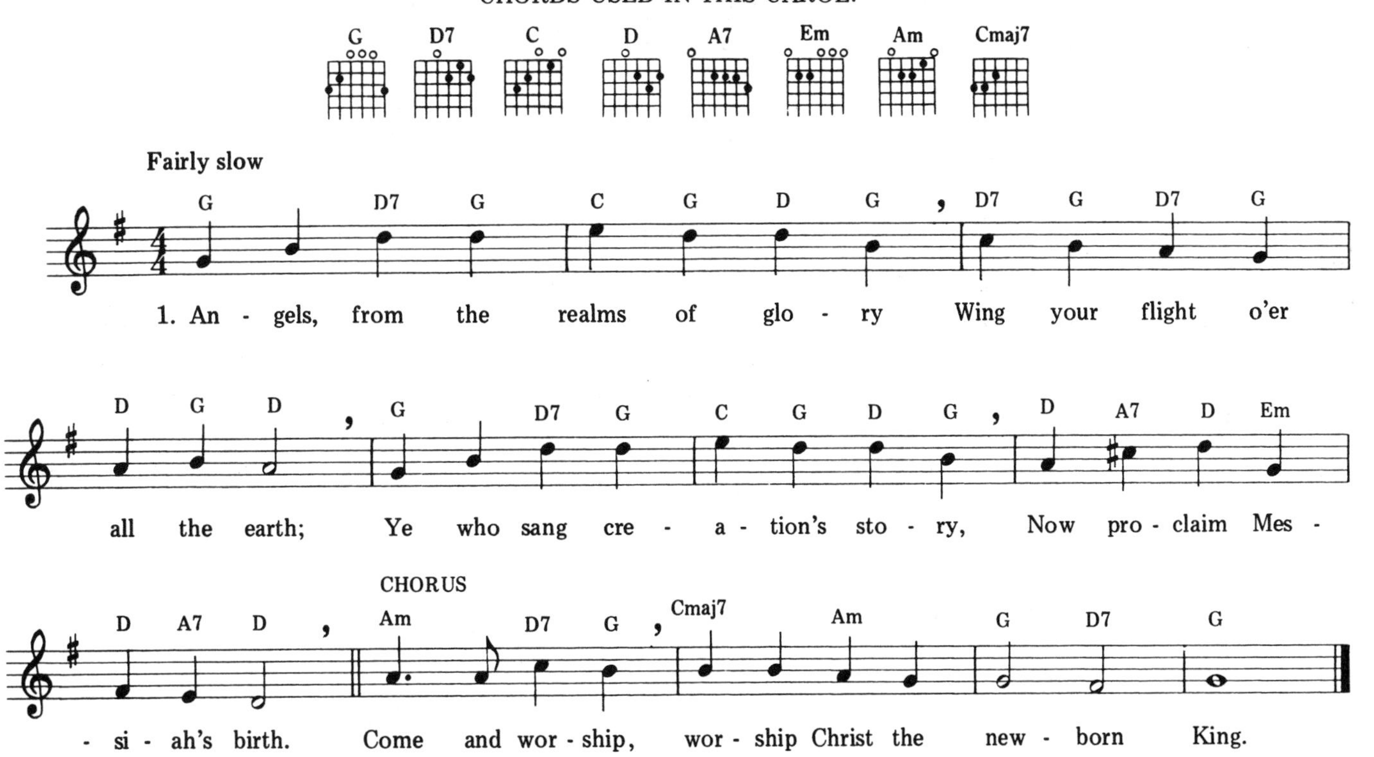

2. Shepherds in the fields abiding,
   Watching o'er your flocks by night;
   God with man is now residing;
   Yonder shines the infant light.
   Come and worship etc.

3. Sages leave your contemplations,
   Brighter visions beam afar;
   Seek the great desire of nations,
   Ye have seen His natal star.
   Come and worship etc.

4. Saints, before the altar bending
   Watching long with hope and fear,
   Suddenly the Lord, descending,
   In His temple shall appear;
   Come and worship etc.

5. Sinner, wrung with true repentance,
   Doomed for guilt to endless pains,
   Justice now revokes the sentence –
   Mercy calls you – break your chains.
   Come and worship etc.

Away In A Manger

CHORDS USED IN THIS CAROL:

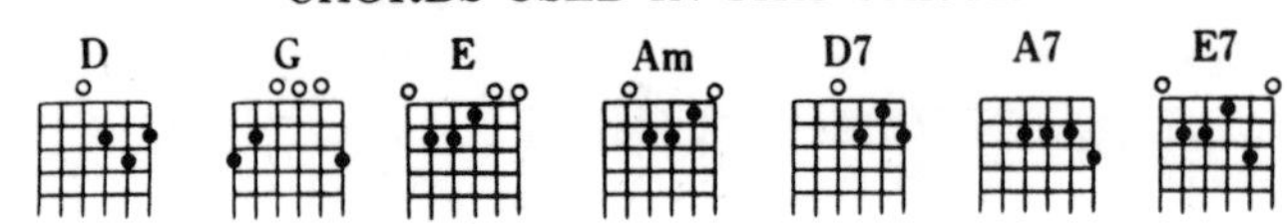

2. The cattle are lowing,
The baby awakes,
But little Lord Jesus,
No crying He makes.
I love Thee, Lord Jesus!
Look down from the sky,
And stay by my side,
Until morning is nigh.

3. Be near me, Lord Jesus;
I ask Thee to stay
Close by me forever,
And love me, I pray.
Bless all the dear children
In Thy tender care,
And fit us for heaven,
To live with Thee there.

Christians, Awake!

CHORDS USED IN THIS CAROL:

2. Then to the watchful shepherds it was told,
Who heard the angelic herald's voice,
"Behold, I bring glad tidings of a Saviour's birth
To you and all the nations upon earth:
This day hath God fulfilled His promised word;
This day is born a Saviour, Christ the Lord!"

3. To Bethlehem straight the enlightened shepherds ran
To see the wonder God had wrought for man,
And found, with Joseph and the Blessed Maid,
Her Son, the Saviour, in a manger laid:
Then to the flocks, still praising God, return,
And their glad hearts with holy rapture burn.

4. O may we keep and ponder in our mind
God's wondrous love in saving lost mankind;
Trace we the Babe, Who hath retrieved our loss,
From His poor manger to His bitter Cross;
Tread in His steps, assisted by His Grace,
Till man's first heavenly state again takes place.

5. Then may we hope, the Angelic hosts among,
To sing, redeemed, a glad triumphal song;
He that was born upon this joyful day
Around us all His glory shall display;
Saved by His love, incessant we shall sing
Eternal praise to heaven's Almighty King.

The Coventry Carol

CHORDS USED IN THIS CAROL:

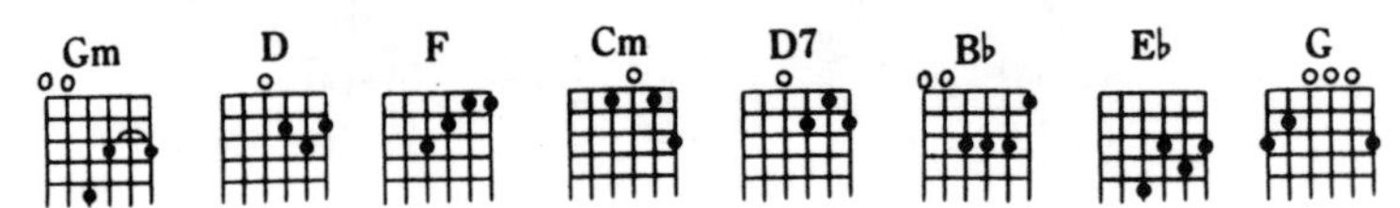

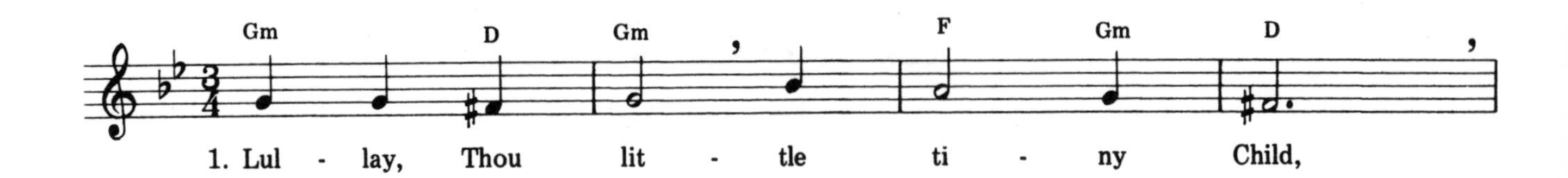

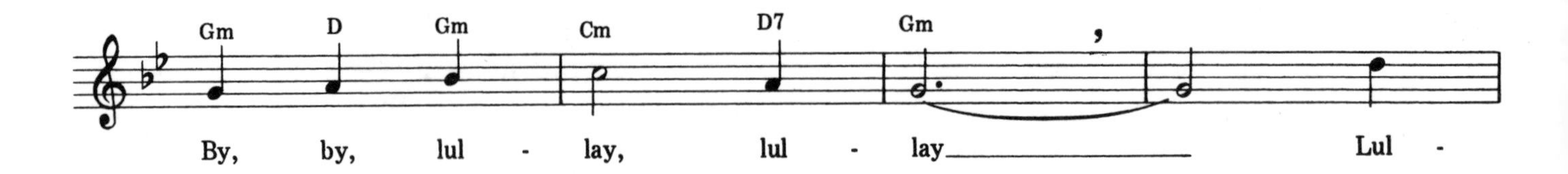

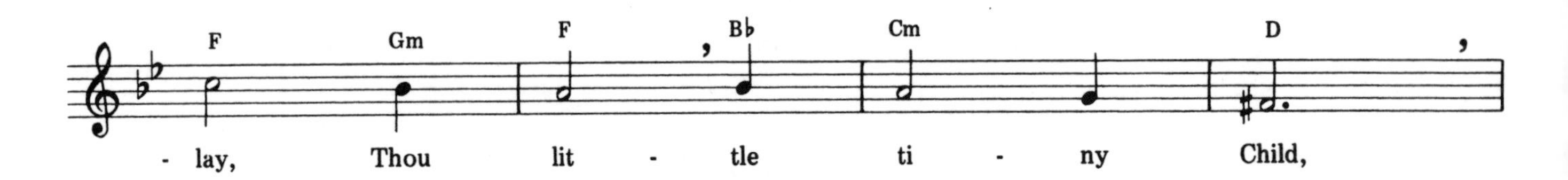

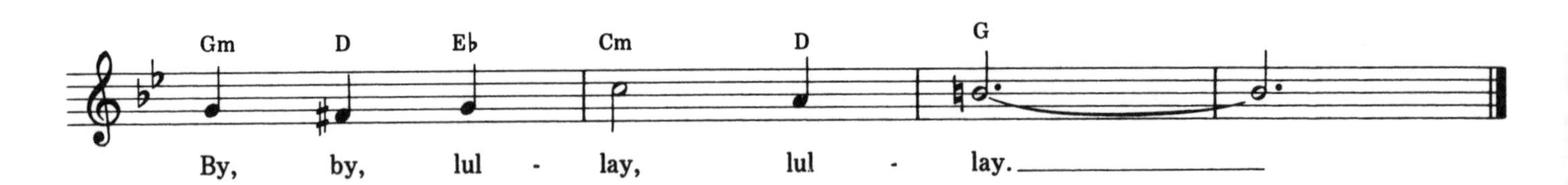

2. O sisters too, how may we do,
   For to preserve this day,
   This poor Youngling for whom we sing,
   By, by, lullay, lullay?

3. Herod the king in his raging,
   Charged he hath this day
   His men of might, in his own sight,
   All children young to slay.

4. Then woe is me, poor Child, for Thee,
   And ever mourn and say,
   For Thy parting nor say nor sing,
   By, by, lullay, lullay.

The First Nowell

CHORDS USED IN THIS CAROL:

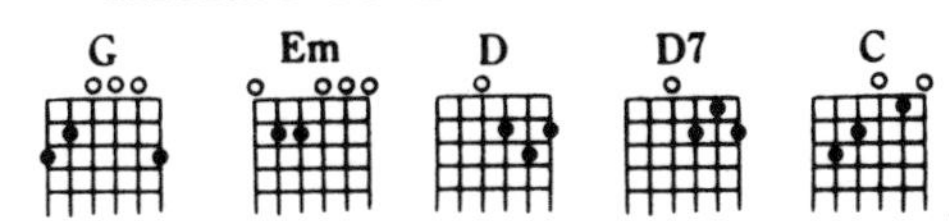

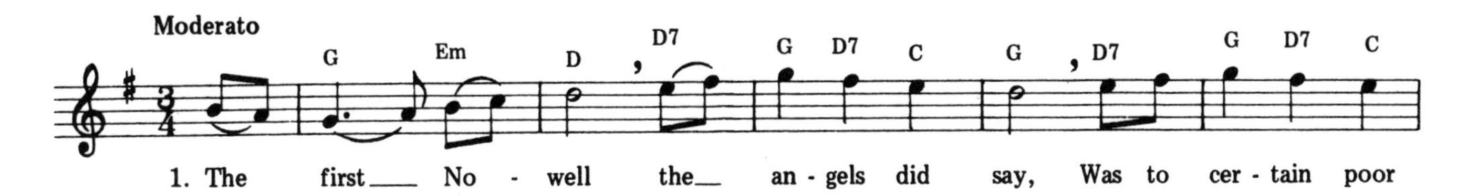

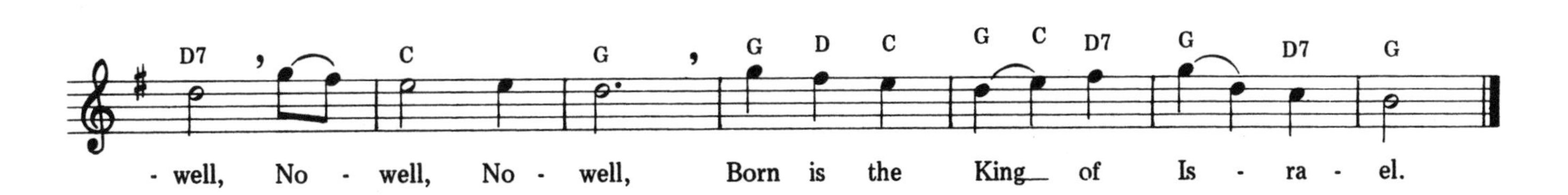

2. They looked up and saw a star,
   Shining in the east beyond them far,
   And to the earth it gave great light,
   And so it continued both day and night.
   Nowell etc.

3. And by the light of that same star,
   Three wise men came from country far;
   To seek for a king was their intent,
   And to follow the star wherever it went.
   Nowell etc.

4. This star drew nigh to the north-west,
   O'er Bethlehem it took its rest,
   And there it did both stop and stay,
   Right over the place where Jesus lay.
   Nowell etc.

5. Then let us all with one accord,
   Sing praises to our heavenly Lord,
   That hath made heaven and earth of nought,
   And with His blood mankind hath bought.
   Nowell etc.

God Rest You Merry Gentlemen

CHORDS USED IN THIS CAROL:

joy, Com-fort and joy; And it's ti - dings of com - fort and joy.

2. From God that is our Father,
The blessed angels came,
Unto some certain shepherds
With tidings of the same;
That there was born in Bethlehem
The son of God by name.
And it's tidings etc.

3. Go, fear not, said God's angels
Let nothing you affright,
For there is born in Bethlehem,
Of a pure Virgin bright,
One able to advance you,
And throw down Satan quite.
And it's tidings etc.

4. The shepherds at those tidings,
Rejoiced much in mind,
And left their flocks a-feeding
In tempest storms of wind,
And straight they came to Bethlehem
The son of God to find.
And it's tidings etc.

5. Now when they came to Bethlehem,
Where our sweet Saviour lay,
They found Him in a manger,
Where oxen feed on hay,
The blessed Virgin kneeling down,
Unto the Lord did pray.
And it's tidings etc.

6. With sudden joy and gladness
The shepherds were beguil'd,
To see the Babe of Israel
Before His mother mild.
On them with joy and cheerfulness
Rejoice each mother's child.
And it's tidings etc.

7. Now to the Lord sing praises,
All you within this place;
Like we true loving brethren,
Each other to embrace,
For the merry time of Christmas
Is drawing on apace.
And it's tidings etc.

Good Christian Men Rejoice

CHORDS USED IN THIS CAROL:

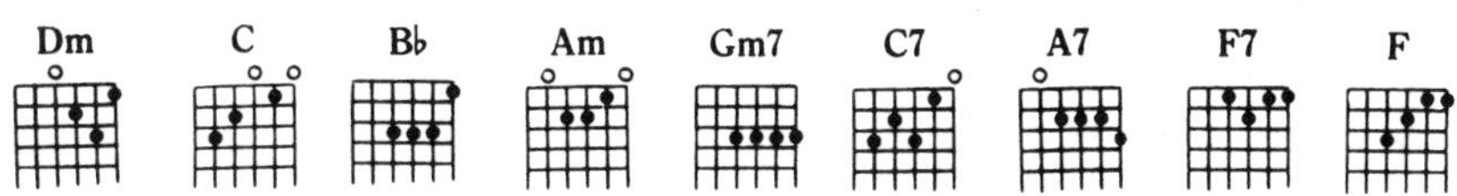

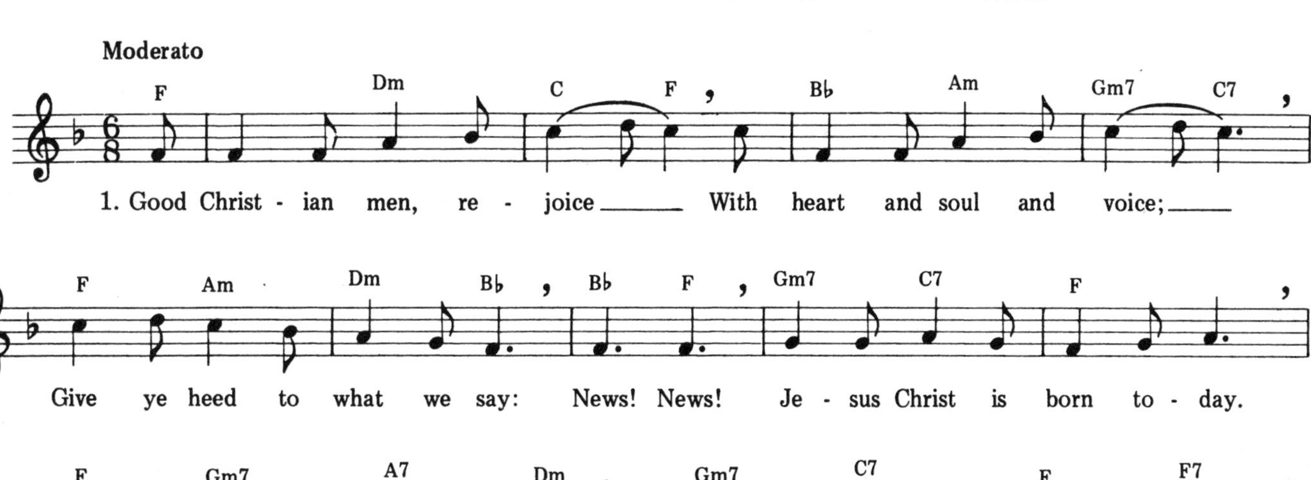

2. Good Christian men, rejoice
With heart and soul and voice;
Now ye hear of endless bliss:
Joy! Joy! Jesus Christ was born for this!
He hath oped the heav'nly door,
And man is blessed evermore.
Christ was born for this!
Christ was born for this!

3. Good Christian men, rejoice
With heart and soul and voice;
Now ye need not fear the grave:
Peace! Peace! Jesus Christ was born to save!
Calls you one and calls you all,
To gain His everlasting hall:
Christ was born to save!
Christ was born to save!

Good King Wenceslas

CHORDS USED IN THIS CAROL:

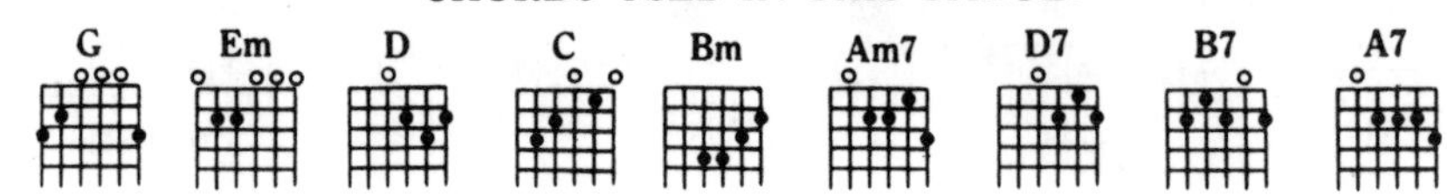

Moderato

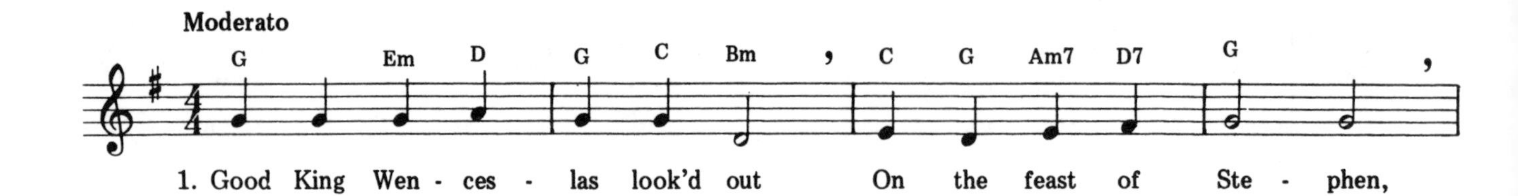

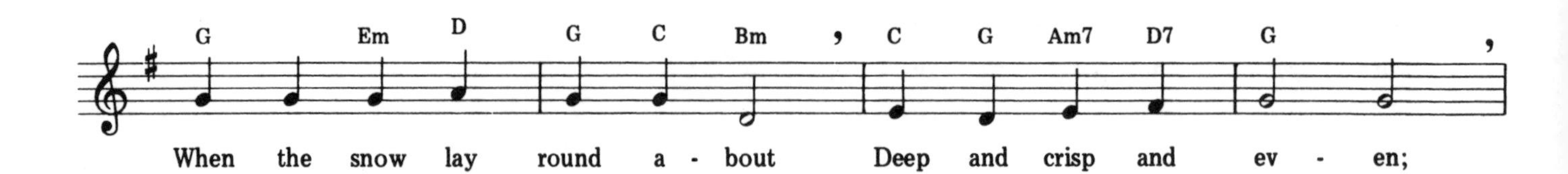

2. "Hither, page, and stand by me,
If thou know'st it, telling,
Yonder peasant, who is he?
Where and what his dwelling?"
"Sire, he lives a good league hence,
Underneath the mountain;
Right against the forest fence,
By Saint Agnes' fountain."

3. "Bring me flesh and bring me wine,
Bring me pine logs hither;
Thou and I will see him dine,
When we bear them thither."
Page and monarch forth they went,
Onward both together,
Through the rude wind's wild lament,
And the bitter weather.

4. "Sire, the night is darker now
And the wind blows stronger;
Fails my heart, I know not how,
I can go no longer."
"Mark my footsteps, good my page!
Tread thou in them boldly;
Thou shall find the winter's rage
Freeze thy blood less coldly."

5. In his master's steps he trod,
Where the snow lay dinted;
Heat was in the very sod
Which the saint had printed.
Therefore, Christian men, be sure –
Wealth or rank possessing –
Ye, who now will bless the poor,
Shall yourselves find blessing.

Hark! The Herald Angels Sing

CHORDS USED IN THIS CAROL:

2. Christ by highest heav'n adored,
   Christ, the everlasting Lord;
   Late in time behold Him come,
   Offspring of a Virgin's womb,
   Veiled in flesh the Godhead see!
   Hail th'incarnate Deity!
   Pleased as man with man to dwell,
   Jesus our Emmanuel.
   Hark! The herald angels sing,
   Glory to the new-born King!

3. Hail, the heaven born Prince of peace!
   Hail, the Son of righteousness!
   Light and life to all He brings,
   Risen with healing in His wings,
   Mild He lays His glory by;
   Born that man no more may die;
   Born to raise the sons of earth;
   Born, to give them second birth.
   Hark! The herald angels sing,
   Glory to the new-born King!

Here We Come A Wassailing

CHORDS USED IN THIS CAROL:

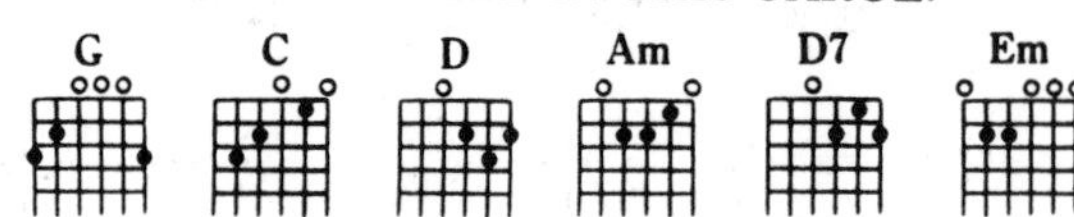

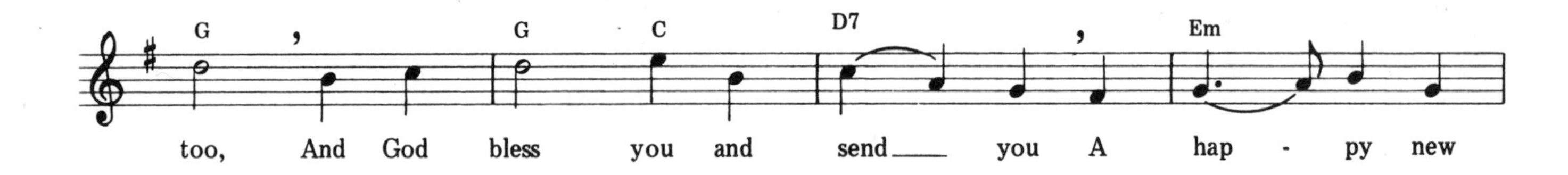

2. We are not daily beggars
   That beg from door to door,
   But we are neighbour's children
   Whom you have seen before.
   Love and Joy etc.

3. Good Master and good Mistress,
   As you sit by the fire,
   Pray think of us poor children
   Who are wand'ring in the mire.
   Love and Joy etc.

4. God bless the Master of this house,
   Likewise the Mistress too;
   And all the little children
   That round the table go.
   Love and Joy etc.

The Holly And The Ivy

CHORDS USED IN THIS CAROL:

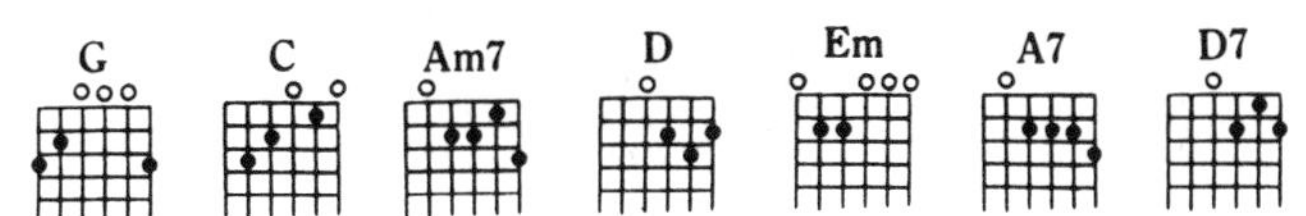

2. The holly bears a blossom,
As white as the lily flower,
And Mary bore sweet Jesus Christ
To be our sweet saviour.
The rising of etc.

3. The holly bears a berry,
As red as any blood,
And Mary bore sweet Jesus Christ
To do poor sinners good.
The rising of etc.

4. The holly bears a prickle,
As sharp as any thorn,
And Mary bore sweet Jesus Christ
On Christmas day in the morn.
The rising of etc.

5. The holly bears a bark,
As bitter as any gall,
And Mary bore sweet Jesus Christ
For to redeem us all.
The rising of etc.

6. The holly and the ivy,
When they are both full grown,
Of all the trees that are in the wood,
The holly bears the crown.
The rising of etc.

The Huron Carol

CHORDS USED IN THIS CAROL:

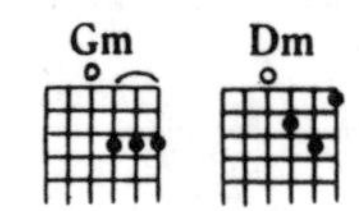

2. Within a lodge of broken bark the tender babe was found.
A ragged robe of rabbit skin enwrapped his beauty round;
And as the hunter braves drew nigh the angel song rang loud and high:
"Jesus your King is born, Jesus is born: In excelsis gloria!"

3. The earliest moon of winter time is not so round and fair.
As was the ring of glory on the helpless infant there.
The chiefs from far before him knelt with gifts of fox and beaver pelt.
"Jesus your King is born, Jesus is born: In excelsis gloria!"

4. O children of the forest free, O, sons of Manitou,
The holy child of earth and heaven is born today for you.
Come kneel before the radiant boy who brings you beauty, peace and joy.
"Jesus your King is born, Jesus is born: In excelsis gloria!"

I Saw Three Ships

CHORDS USED IN THIS CAROL:

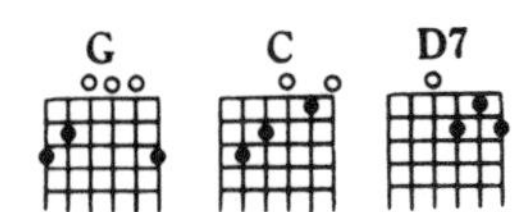

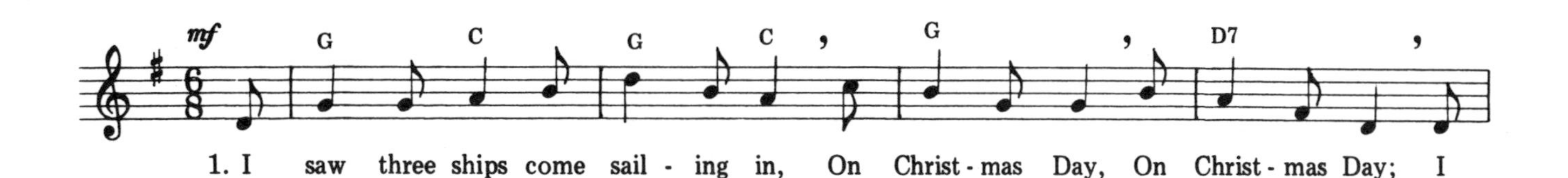

2. And what was in those ships all three,
   On Christmas day, on Christmas day?
   And what was in those ships all three,
   On Christmas day in the morning?

3. Our Saviour Christ and His lady,
   On Christmas day, on Christmas day;
   Our Saviour Christ and His lady,
   On Christmas day in the morning.

4. Pray, whither sailed those ships all three,
   On Christmas day, on Christmas day?
   Pray, whither sailed those ships all three,
   On Christmas day in the morning?

5. O they sailed into Bethlehem,
   On Christmas day, on Christmas day;
   O they sailed into Bethlehem,
   On Christmas day in the morning.

6. And all the bells on earth shall ring,
   On Christmas day, on Christmas day;
   And all the bells on earth shall ring,
   On Christmas day in the morning.

7. And all the Angels in Heaven shall sing,
   On Christmas day, on Christmas day;
   And all the Angels in Heaven shall sing,
   On Christmas day in the morning.

8. And all the souls on earth shall sing,
   On Christmas day, on Christmas day;
   And all the souls on earth shall sing,
   On Christmas day in the morning.

9. Then let us all rejoice amain,
   On Christmas day, on Christmas day;
   Then let us all rejoice amain,
   On Christmas day in the morning.

Amazing Grace

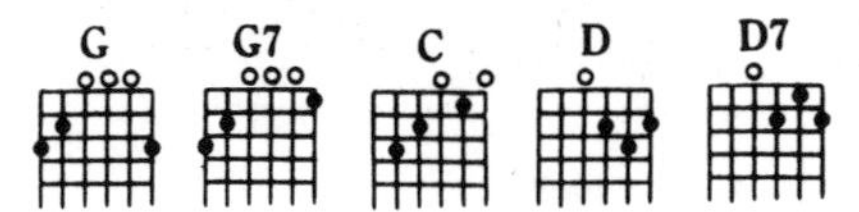

Traditional

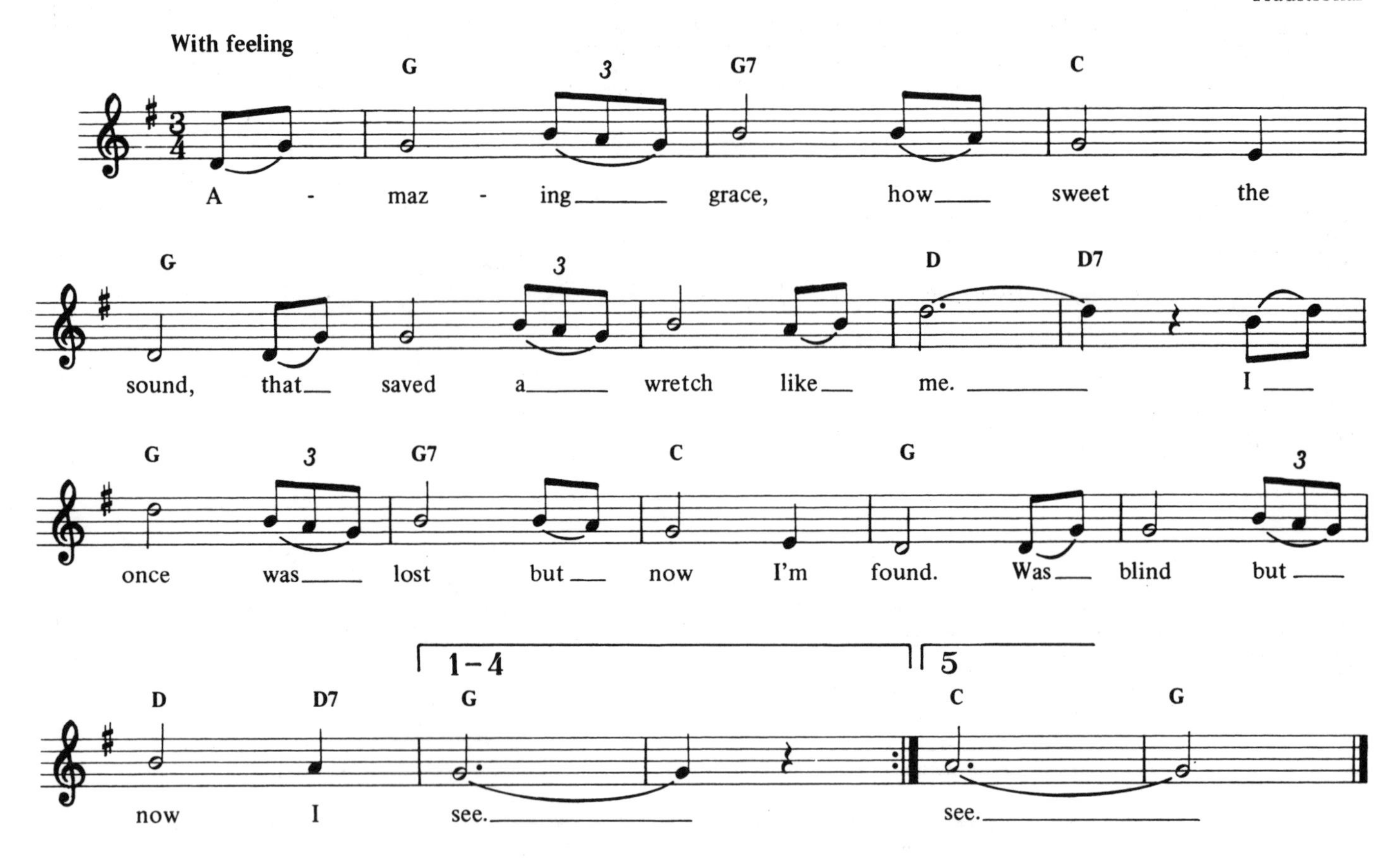

2 'Twas grace that taught my heart to fear
And grace, my fears relieved.
How precious did that grace appear,
The hour I first believed.

3 Through many dangers toils and snares
We have already come.
'Twas grace that brought me safe thus far,
And grace will lead me home.

4 When we've been there ten thousand years
Bright shining as the sun.
We've no less days to sing God's praise
Than when we first begun.

5 Amazing grace how sweet the sound
That saved a wretch like me
I once was lost but now I'm found
Was blind but now I see.

It Came Upon The Midnight Clear

CHORDS USED IN THIS CAROL:

2. Still through the cloven skies they come
With peaceful wings unfurled;
And still their heavenly music floats
O'er all the weary world:
Above its sad and lowly plains
They bend on heavenly wing,
And ever o'er its Babel sounds
The blessed angels sing.

3. Yet with the woes of sin and strife
The world has suffered long;
Beneath the angel-strain have rolled
Two thousand years of wrong;
And men, at war with men, hear not
The words of peace they bring:
Oh, listen now, ye men of strife,
And hear the angels sing.

4. O Prince of Peace, Thou knowest well
This weary world below;
Thou seest how men climb the way
With painful steps and slow,
Oh, still the jarring sounds of earth
That through the pathway ring,
And bid the toilers rest awhile
To hear the angels sing.

Jingle Bells

CHORDS USED IN THIS SONG:

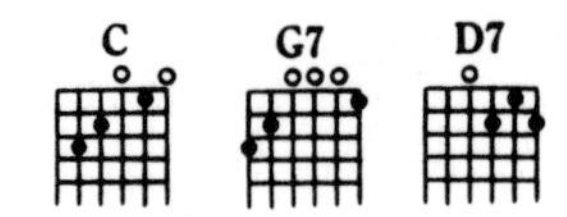

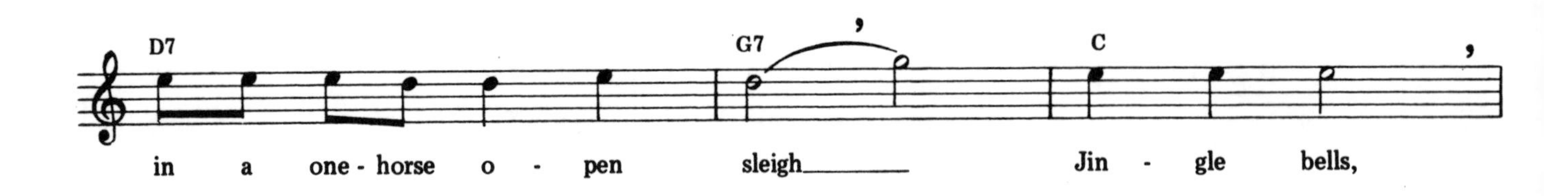

Kumbaya

CHORDS USED IN THIS SONG:

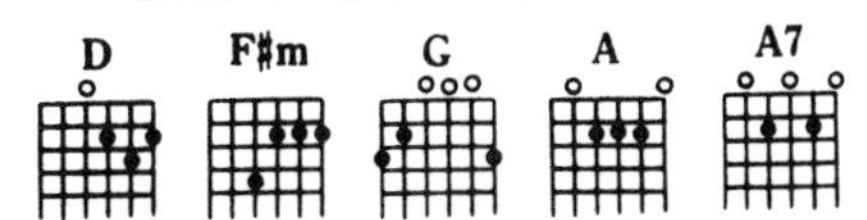

Traditional

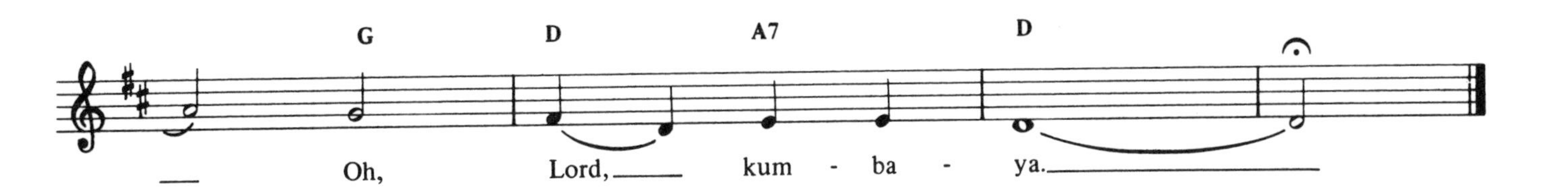

2 Someone's singing, Lord, kumbaya (3)
Oh, Lord, kumbaya.

3 Someone's praying, Lord, kumbaya (3)
Oh, Lord, kumbaya.

4 Kumbaya, my Lord, kumbaya (3)
Oh, Lord, kumbaya.

O Come, All Ye Faithful

CHORDS USED IN THIS CAROL:

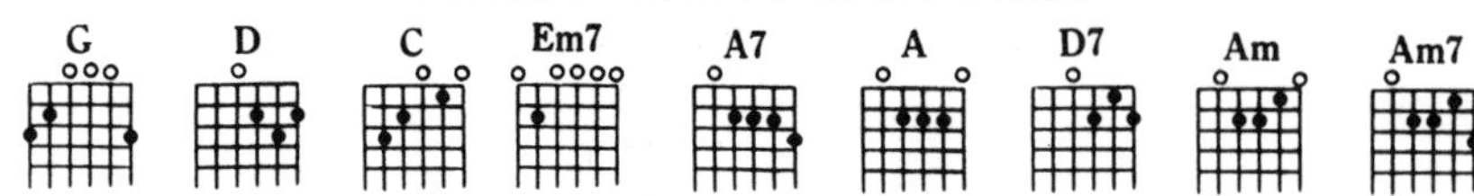

2. God of God,
Light of Light,
Lo, He abhors not the Virgin's womb,
Very God, begotten not created:
O come, let us etc.

3. Sing, choirs of Angels,
Sing in exultation,
Sing, all ye citizens of heav'n above:
'Glory to God in the highest;'
O come, let us etc.

4. Yea, Lord, we greet Thee,
Born this happy morning;
Jesu, to Thee be glory given;
Word of the Father, Now in flesh appearing;
O come, let us etc.

He's Got The Whole World In His Hands

2 He's got the land and sea in His hands;
He's got the night and day in His hands;
He's got the spring and fall in His hands;
He's got the whole world in His hands.

3 He's got the young and old in His hands;
He's got the rich and poor in His hands;
He's got everyone in His hands;
He's got the whole world in His hands.

Once In Royal David's City

CHORDS USED IN THIS CAROL:

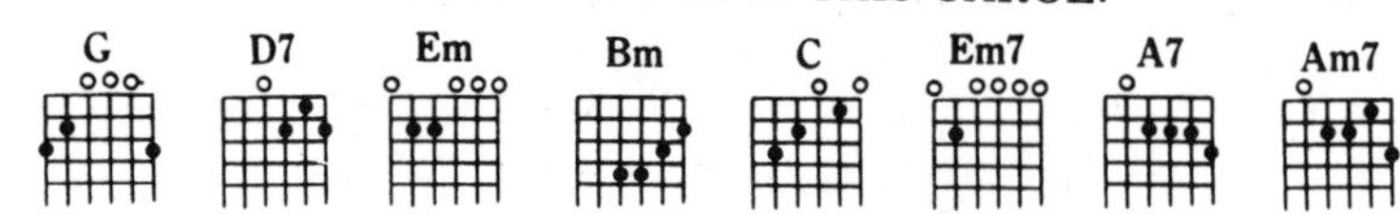

Moderato

2. He came down to earth from Heaven
   Who is God and Lord of all,
   And His shelter was a stable,
   And His cradle was a stall;
   With the poor, the mean, and lowly,
   Lived on earth our Saviour Holy.

3. And through all His wondrous childhood,
   He would honour and obey,
   Love and watch the lowly Maiden
   In whose gentle arms He lay;
   Christian children all must be
   Mild, obedient, good as He.

4. For He is in our childhood's pattern,
   Day by day like us He grew;
   He was little, weak and helpless,
   Tears and smiles like us He knew;
   And He feeleth for our sadness,
   And He shareth in our gladness.

5. And our eyes at last shall see Him,
   Through His own redeeming love,
   For that Child so dear and gentle
   Is our Lord in heaven above;
   And he leads His children on
   To the place where He is gone.

6. Not in that poor lowly stable,
   With the oxen standing by,
   We shall see Him; but in heaven,
   Set at God's right hand on high;
   When like stars his children crown'd
   All in white shall wait around.

See Amid The Winter's Snow

CHORDS USED IN THIS CAROL:

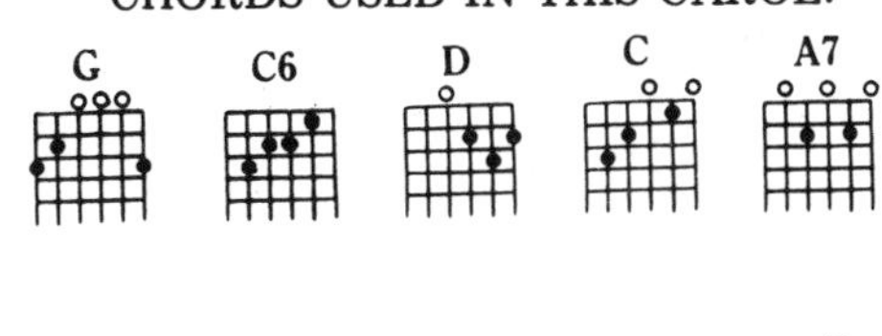

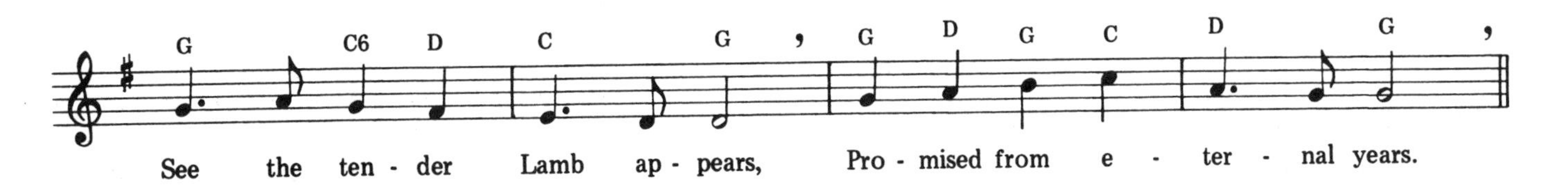

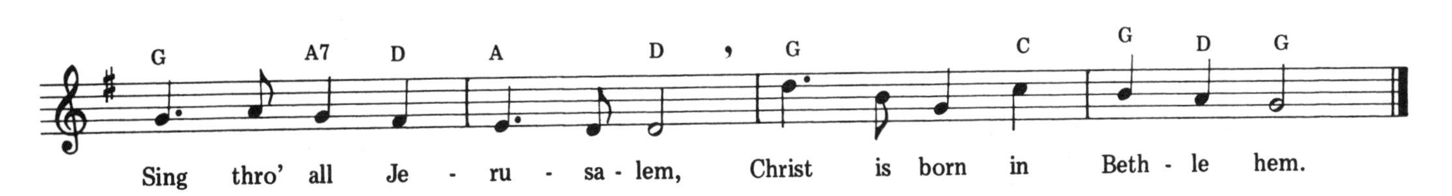

2. Lo, within a manger lies
   He who built the starry skies;
   He, who throned in height sublime,
   Sits amid the Cherubim!
   Hail, thou ever-blessed, etc.

3. Say, ye holy Shepherds, say,
   What your joyful news to-day;
   Wherefore have ye left your sheep
   On the lonely mountain steep?
   Hail, thou ever-blessed, etc.

4. "As we watched at dead of night,
   Lo, we saw a wondrous light;
   Angels singing peace on earth,
   Told us of a Saviour's Birth."
   Hail, thou ever-blessed, etc.

5. Sacred Infant, all Divine,
   What a tender love was Thine;
   Thus to come from highest bliss
   Down to such a world as this!
   Hail, thou ever-blessed, etc.

6. Teach, O teach us, Holy Child,
   By Thy face so meek and mild,
   Teach us to resemble Thee,
   In Thy sweet humility!
   Hail, thou ever-blessed, etc.

Silent Night

CHORDS USED IN THIS CAROL:

2. Silent night! Holy night!
Shepherds quail at the sight,
Glories stream from heav'n afar,
Heav'nly hosts sing Alleluia!
Christ the Saviour is born,
Christ the Saviour is born.

3. Silent night! Holy night!
Son of God, love's pure light;
Radiant beams Thy holy face
With the dawn of saving grace,
Jesus, Lord, at Thy birth,
Jesus, Lord, at Thy birth.

Unto Us A Boy Is Born

CHORDS USED IN THIS CAROL:

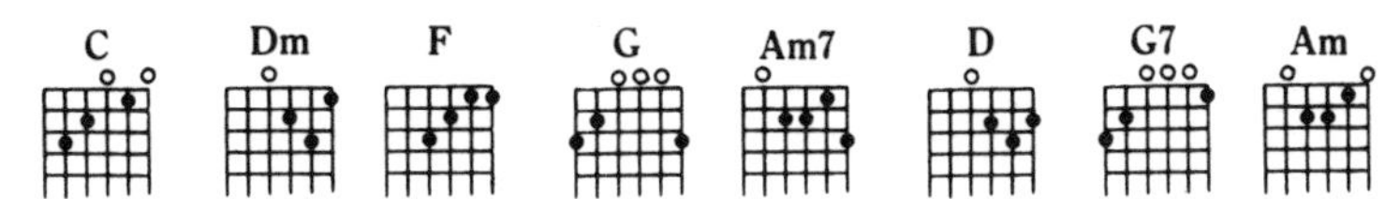

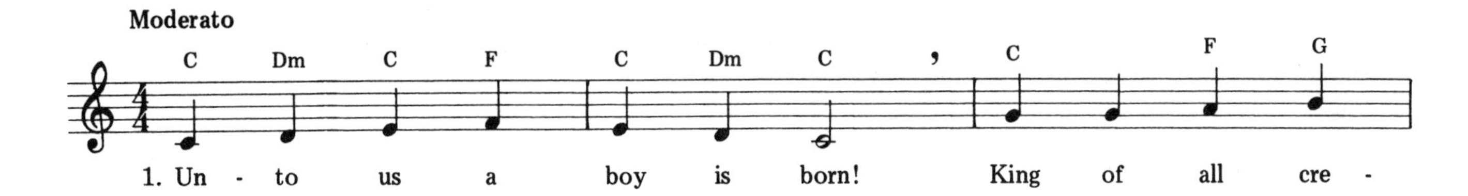

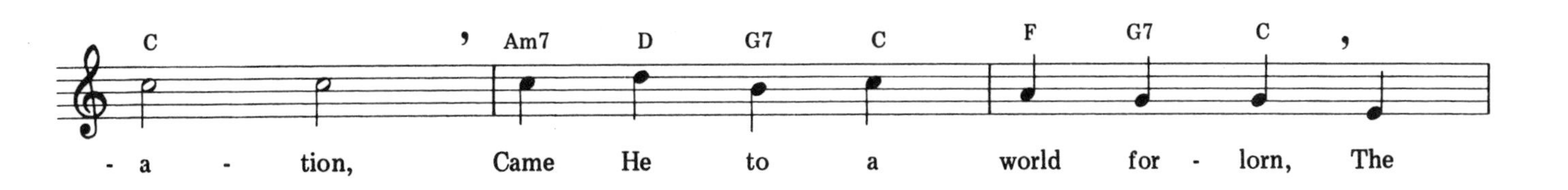

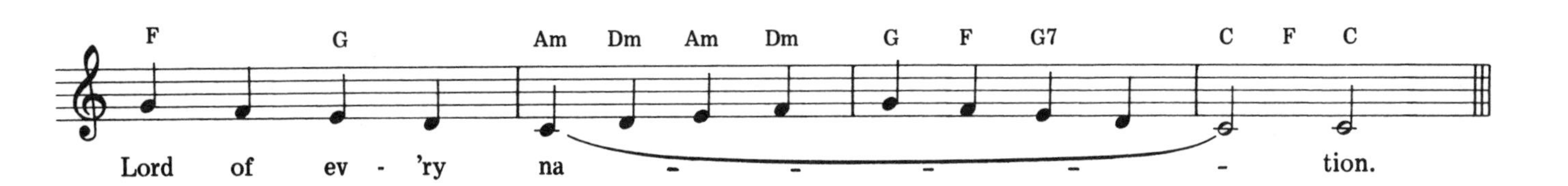

2. Cradled in a stall was He
With sleepy cows and asses;
But the very beasts could see
That He all men surpasses.

3. Herod then with fear was filled:
"A prince", he said, "in Jewry!"
All the little boys he killed
At Bethlem in his fury.

4. Now may Mary's son, who came
So long ago to love us,
Lead us all with hearts aflame
Unto the joys above us.

5. Omega and Alpha He!
Let the organ thunder,
While the choir with peals of glee
Doth rend the air asunder.

We Three Kings

(Melchior)

2. Born a king on Bethlehem plain,
Gold I bring to crown him again,
King for ever, ceasing never,
Over us all to reign.
O star of wonder etc.

(Caspar)

3. Frankincense to offer have I;
Incense owns a Deity nigh:
Prayer and praising, all men raising,
Worship him, God most high.
O star of wonder etc.

(Balthazar)

4. Myrrh is mine; its bitter perfume
Breathes a life of gathering gloom;
Sorrowing, sighing, bleeding, dying,
Sealed in the stone-cold tomb.
O star of wonder etc.

(All)

5. Glorious now, behold him arise,
King and God and Sacrifice!
Heaven sings alleluya,
Alleluya the earth replies.
O star of wonder etc.

We Wish You A Merry Christmas

CHORDS USED IN THIS CAROL:

2. Now bring us some figgy pudding,
Now bring us some figgy pudding,
Now bring us some figgy pudding,
And bring some out here.
Good tidings etc.

3. For we all like figgy pudding,
For we all like figgy pudding,
For we all like figgy pudding,
So bring some out here.
Good tidings etc.

4. And we won't go till we've got some,
And we won't go till we've got some,
And we won't go till we've got some,
So bring some out here.
Good tidings etc.

While Shepherds Watched Their Flocks

CHORDS USED IN THIS CAROL:

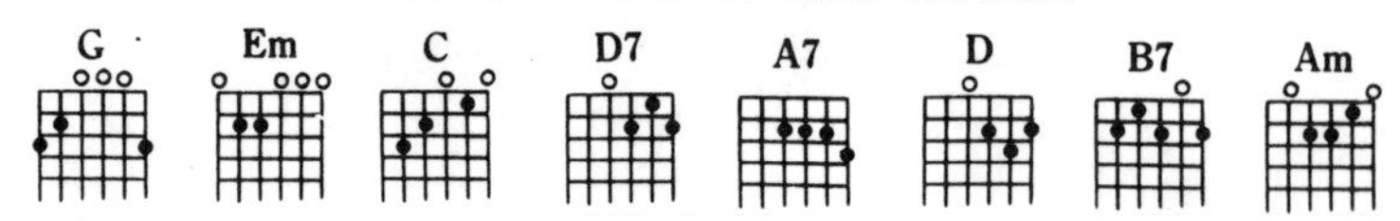

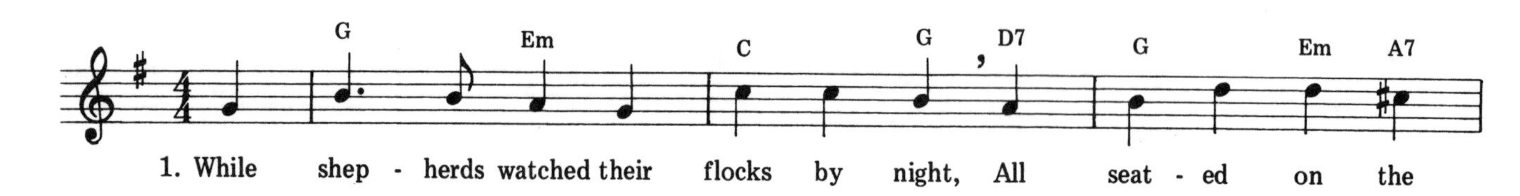

2. "Fear not," said he; for mighty dread
Had seized their troubled mind;
"Glad tidings of great joy I bring
To you and all mankind."

3. "To you in David's town this day
Is born of David's line
A Saviour, who is Christ the Lord;
And this shall be the sign:"

4. "The heavenly Babe you there shall find
To human view display'd,
All meanly wrapp'd in swathing bands,
And in a manger laid."

5. Thus spake the seraph; and forthwith
Appeared a shining throng
Of angels praising God, who thus
Addressed their joyful song:

6. "All glory be to God on high,
And on the earth be peace;
Good-will henceforth from heaven to men
Begin and never cease."

8/05(55694)
Printed in England